NUNS – WHAT ARE THEY FOR?

Comprising

CONTEMPLATIVE NUNS: ARE THEY WASTING THEIR LIVES?

Maria Boulding OSB

1973

WHY ENCLOSED NUNS?

Dom Bruno Webb OSB

1951

NUNS – WHAT IS SPECIAL ABOUT THEM?

Jean Cardinal Daniélou SJ

1974

CATHOLIC TRUTH SOCIETY

PUBLISHERS TO THE HOLY SEE

The essential "work"
of a contemplative nun
is to commit herself
with all her being to the love
and worship of God.

Maria Boulding (1929-2009) was a nun of Stanbrook Abbey;
Bruno Webb (ob. 1976) was a monk of Prinknash;
Jean Daniélou (1905-1974) an eminent Jesuit theologian.

CTS ONEFIFTIES
Originally published as *Contemplative Nuns: are they wasting their lives?*, 1973;
Why Enclosed Nuns? 1951; *Nuns – what is special about them?* 1974.
Published by The Incorporated Catholic Truth Society,
40-46 Harleyford Road, London SE11 5AY
www.ctsbooks.org
Copyright © 2017 The Incorporated Catholic Truth Society.

ISBN 978 1 78469 536 1

CONTEMPLATIVE NUNS:
are they wasting their lives?

Sr Maria Boulding OSB

CONTEMPLATIVE NUNS
are they wasting their lives?

Sr Maria Boulding OSB

One day certain fishermen had to admit that they hadn't been doing too well. It was not that they lacked skill or experience, but there is a certain amount of luck in these things, and it was not their lucky day – or their lucky night either, for it had been an all-night job and the results had been nil. Then a friend sitting in one of the boats said, 'Put out into deep water and drop the nets there.' It didn't seem like very good advice; the speaker was not himself a fisherman and could hardly be expected to know much about it. But there was something about *him* that called forth a highly personal response, a response of trust and commitment and love, so the leading fisherman replied, 'We slaved all night and it was no good – but if *you* say so, I'll do it.' He did, and the catch was so heavy that it took the combined strength of his partners to get it ashore safely.[1]

PERSONAL CALL AND RESPONSE

Choosing to follow

That story concerns the apostles, but probably most contemplative nuns would recognise in it the elements of their own vocation: a call of grace to 'launch out into the deep' away from what is familiar and controllable, a free decision to do so on the word of the one who calls, and some kind of certainty that this commitment to a venture which

[1] Lk 5:1–11.

does not seem to make sense leads to a life of enormous fruitfulness for the Church.

This is not to say that a vocation to the contemplative life begins with some sort of special 'spiritual experience'; few nuns would claim that in their case it did. God can grasp a person through any kind of human experience and his ways of making his will known are very various. He often makes use of the intelligence and common sense he has himself created in us. But however the call is made known, it is always a personal grace demanding a fully personal, human, free response. The mainspring of the response is love, which is itself the work of grace and yet truly our own.

Contemporary philosophies have helped us to understand how much the human person grows and becomes himself through free decision. A young child is open to many possibilities and committed to none, but as he approaches adulthood he has to decide what to do with his life, and the very word 'decide' comes from the Latin word *de-cidere*, to cut away. So to decide on any good thing means cutting away and sacrificing not only bad things but many other good alternatives that are not compatible with what we choose. And the more total our dedication to the good thing we feel called to choose, the greater will be the sacrifices entailed. There are plenty of instances of this in today's society; astronauts for example have to undergo rigorous training and give up many other enjoyable and interesting pursuits for the sake of the supreme effort they are to make in the service of science.

In our life with God a radical option may be asked of us that entails renunciation of many other good things – ways of serving God and the Church and mankind, or possibilities of human development. A girl or young woman whom God calls to be a contemplative nun has to make such a choice. She can do it only through living personal faith in the God whose word has come to her and will continue to call her throughout her life. This is a very direct and personal obedience to the will of God as she has discovered it, and it is the foundation of all the obedience she will have to practise in her religious life. It implies too a self-acceptance and an acknowledgement of her own limitations; she cannot do everything, orient her life in all directions at once, and follow every kind of worth-while career, so what matters is that she should do wholeheartedly what God asks of her, leaving him to see that her life serves his purpose.

A new exodus

She makes herself fully available to God, and in order to do so she goes into the desert. This is another biblical theme. God called the Hebrews out of Egypt when he wanted to make them his own people and pledged himself in love to them through the covenant. He called individuals into the desert at important times to renew this experience of intimacy with God.[1] Jesus was 'driven' by the Spirit into the desert to confront God and himself after the experience of his baptism and before taking up his messianic work.[2] Every Christian undergoes this personal exodus in some way: our baptism is a breaking free from the life of the 'old man' or the slavery of Egypt, and on Easter night we celebrate our new exodus in Christ. A contemplative nun is called to follow Christ into the desert in a particular way, that with him she may listen to the word of God and be open to the Spirit. The monastery is her desert; she enters it in faith and love and repentance, not knowing what God will give or ask. She simply says 'Yes' to God.

As time passes she grows more deeply into the mystery of this life she has entered. She has chosen silence and stillness, yet these are somehow more powerful than all feverish activity. She has given up everything that is supposed to make life worth living, yet she finds a joy and fullness of life that she did not know before. She sets out alone, and yet finds that in a community where there is 'one heart and one soul' and where 'everything is held in common'[3] she is discovering the mysterious union of all believers in Christ; her life is a strange blend of aloneness with God and joyful communion with others, and these things are not contradictory because both stem from love. She seeks God daily in prayer, increasingly aware of her emptiness and inability to pray but at the same time convinced that prayer matters above all and that it is

---

[1] I Kgs 19; cf Hos 2:16–25; Lk 1:80.
[2] Mk 1:12.
[3] Acts 4:32.

more God's work than hers. Her prayer is a lonely, dark path through a wilderness, yet there is an inexplicable certainty that God understands, and every day at Mass and in the office she is one with the members of a worshipping community who are drawn in their common prayer into closest union with God and one another. She gives herself to God in love and fidelity, discovering her own weakness and need of his mercy and yet finding that this very poverty of spirit is somehow a help.

Why enclosure?

Withdrawal from some of the noise and turmoil of modern living is necessary if a life like this is to be real, for concentration is a condition for any great undertaking. Enclosure has to some extent characterised the life of nuns from earliest times. It is a sign and guarantee of their renunciation of aspects of life that are merely this-worldly, and it helps to keep them free for the work they are called to do. Since the Council of Trent it has often been symbolised by grilles, but grilles are not essential to enclosure and recent directives of the Church have paid more attention to local cultural conditions.[1] A nun does not choose enclosure for its own sake; she cannot love something negative. The closer she is to God the more she will love all whom he loves and whom his Son came to save. But she may know that the renunciations implied by enclosed religious life are part of her vocation, the other side of the coin.

Mere entrance into an enclosed contemplative monastery is, however, not an automatic recipe for holiness. Any profession has its occupational hazards, and the life of enclosed nuns is no exception: selfishness, pettiness, narrowness of mind and the possibility of remaining immature are not excluded by locked doors but only by an ever-renewed willingness to hear the word of God that calls us forth from ourselves. Another characteristic hazard is what the ancient monks called *acedia*, a kind of desperate boredom and dullness to the

---

[1]'The papal cloister for nuns totally dedicated to contemplation is to be retained. Still, it should be modified according to conditions of time and place, and outdated customs done away with. In such matters, consideration should be given to the wishes of the monasteries themselves.' Vatican II, *Perfectae Caritatis*, 16.

things of God. The only cure for this is a deepening in faith. Someone has said that if we are bored in the desert, at any rate there is no doubt about who the bore is.

There is a common misconception that life in a contemplative community is defined by heroic abstention from work. Anyone who tries it with this in mind will be disappointed. The conditions of enclosure generally exclude a visible external apostolate such as teaching or nursing, but regular hard work, whether manual or mental, forms part of the programme of all contemplative communities. Pope Pius XII's Apostolic Constitution *Sponsa Christi* reminded contemplatives of their duty to earn their living, and even where economic pressures do not make it inevitable contemplative nuns are aware of their solidarity with all mankind in this duty to work. St Benedict made manual labour an essential element in monastic life, and most other founders of orders living in a contemplative style have followed him. Apart from services to the community and the upkeep of the house, various forms of service for others, such as making altar breads, arts, crafts, printing and translating, can be carried on in an enclosed community. Hospitality is also a significant form of work in many houses. None of these activities are undertaken for their own sake, however, and the essential apostolate of the contemplative life is independent of them. Enclosed nuns find their apostolate summed up in the words of Vatican II: 'Fired by the love which the Holy Spirit pours out into their hearts, they live their lives increasingly for Christ and for his Body which is the Church. Consequently, the more fervent their union with Christ through this giving of themselves, which includes the whole of their lives, the richer the life of the Church becomes and the more fruitful her apostolate'.[1]

Dedication by vows: does a life-commitment make sense?
The essential 'work' of a contemplative nun is therefore to commit herself with all her being to the love and worship of God. In this love affair God has all the initiative, but by the power of his Spirit she is slowly fashioned into a lover. She loses her life to find it; she gives

---

[1] *Perfectae Caritatis* 1.

herself away to God who created her and grows into a new freedom. Her commitment to him is rooted in her baptism and is reaffirmed in the vows by which her life is taken up into the one sacrifice of Christ.

A life-commitment so total, often undertaken early in life, is thought by many in the unstable society of today to be humanly impossible. In the second half of the twentieth century people are increasingly aware of the contingency, uncertainty and impermanence of human existence, and if there is one value that is generally honoured it is authenticity in one's personal life at every stage. How can it be possible, then, to vow one's whole life to God at 25 or so, and to preserve simultaneously in the years that follow both constant fidelity to one's pledged word *and* authenticity as one grows and changes?

The answer can only be our Lord's answer to the apostles' question after the rich young man had turned away: 'With men it *is* impossible, but not with God.'[1] When a nun makes her profession she is risking everything into the hands of God, believing that he has called her and is still calling her, that he wants this adventure, that though she cannot see into the future and know how she will feel in 40 years' time, *he* can see *now* all that she will become. So her vocation is not something that happens only at the beginning; it is an ongoing relationship in which God gives himself and asks her to surrender herself unreservedly in return. She can be faithful to her vows because 'God is faithful'[2] but this fidelity will be not something static but a deepening and more costly commitment, a continuing 'Yes' to all that was implicit in the initial self-giving, a consent to be used by God, in ways obscure and mysterious to herself, in his plan of salvation.

CONTEMPLATIVE LIFE IN THE CHURCH

The Church as a Body

When Jesus was trying to tell the apostles what the innermost essence of the Church and of salvation was like, he told them he was the vine, and

[1] Mk 10:27.
[2] I Cor. 1:9.

they were its branches[1]. Their business was to remain organically united to him in order that his life might course freely through them and all their activity. This organic union was to be maintained and increased by love and faith, and only in the measure that it remained a living reality would their lives be fruitful. St Paul (who was a townsman and on the whole not as fond of agricultural parables as our Lord was) preferred to teach the same message in terms of a body with its diversified organs: 'The body is one but its parts are many, yet all together form one body, and it is the same with Christ.'[2] Modern evolutionary thinking has perhaps helped us to understand St Paul better. Living organisms, as they ascend from the most primitive forms to mammals and man, display increasing complexity and diversification in the structure and function of their organs, but the more complex they are the more powerful the principle of co-ordination and unity; we have only to think of the almost unimaginable co-ordination achieved through the human brain. So, St Paul goes on to show, it is right that there should be apostles, prophets, teachers, administrators and the rest in the Church, for these are like the eyes, ears, hands and feet of the body. The body needs them all and each part needs the others. Their functions are different but all necessary, and all make for the vitality of the whole body provided that they truly work in response to the one Spirit who animates it.[3] The body is Christ, and Christ's mysteries are lived out in fullness only in the whole Church. No single one of us is big enough to be Christ. But through the members of his Church, Christ who prayed constantly to his Father, often at night, Christ who preached, healed, taught and suffered, continues his saving mysteries in space and time.

'Love at the heart'
But there is one 'function' or gift in the body which is vital above all, and without which its whole activity would be sterile and useless, and that is love. All prophetic powers, wisdom, almsgiving, even martyrdom, St Paul teaches, would be futile if love were not the life-force that

---

[1] Jn 15.
[2] I Cor. 12:12 ff.
[3] I Cor 12:4–11.

energised in them.[1] This was the truth that dawned on St Teresa of the Child Jesus and gave her the key to her vocation: 'I understood that the most necessary, the most noble organ would not be missing in the body of the Church. I understood that the Church had a heart and that this heart was on fire with love. I understood that love alone makes the members of the Church act, and that if love were lacking the apostles would no longer preach the Gospel, and the martyrs no longer shed their blood…. Yes, I have found my place in the Church…at the heart of the Church, I will be love….'[2] This is the universal apostolate of contemplatives, to be love at the heart of the Church. In an address to nuns in July 1962, Pope John reminded them of it: 'The contribution of the contemplatives is so important to the apostolate that Pope Pius XI chose as co-patron of the missions, on equal terms with St Francis Xavier, not a sister of an active order but a Carmelite, St Teresa of the Child Jesus. Yes, all the needs of the Church Militant ought to find a place in your minds and hearts. To no disaster, no struggle or calamity, should you be strangers; no scientific discovery, no phase of culture, no social or political movement should make you think, "These things do not concern us." Let the Church feel that you are present wherever your spiritual contribution is required for the good of souls and for true human progress and universal peace.'

Contemplative communities receive huge numbers of requests for prayer for specific needs, from people known or unknown to them. Intercession for the needs of all mankind is part of their business. Even in the Old Testament the prayer of a man of God prevailed in times of disaster.[3] Under the New Covenant we have our Lord's guarantee that our prayer will be heard: 'Whatever you ask the Father in my name he will give you.'[4] The answer may not always come at the time or in the way that we expect. But whether the intentions are publicly mentioned at Mass or in the office or whether the sisters simply bear these needs in their hearts as they stand before God in prayer, there is a heightening

---

[1] I Cor 13.
[2] Letter to Sister Marie of the Sacred Heart.
[3] e.g. Abraham's, Gen 18:22–32; Moses', Ex 17:8–16, 32:9–14.
[4] Jn 16:23.

of the conscious realisation of our union with one another in the Spirit of the risen Christ.

Living the paschal mystery

But such an involvement in the mystery of salvation 'at the heart of the Church' cannot be a matter only of interest or even loving concern, it must be lived. Salvation is achieved in the cross and resurrection of Christ, and though he won a superabundant redemption he cares enough about our dignity and freedom to want us as his collaborators in the work his Father gave him to do. 'I fill up in my body what is wanting to the sufferings of Christ', says St Paul, 'for his body which is the Church.'[1] In one sense nothing can be wanting, but in another sense Christ waits for us to pray, love and suffer with him and in him. And he gives us his Spirit, so that just as he, rising from the dead, 'lives unto God',[2] we too 'may live no longer for ourselves but for him who died and rose again for us.'[3] This is the responsibility of all Christians. The life of contemplative nuns is an effort to bear that responsibility; their life is 'hidden with Christ in God' in the mystery of Easter.[4]

Speaking of his approaching death, Jesus compared himself to the wheat grain, a single grain at first, but destined to fall into the ground and die and so give life to a plentiful harvest.[5] The same law of life-out-of-death holds good for his disciples, and for the Church as a whole as she is born of the paschal dying and rising of Christ. She asks of the Lord what Rachel asked of Jacob: 'Give me children',[6] but she knows that only by consenting to the paschal mystery will she be fruitful. At this level the most real fecundity of the contemplative life in the Church is to be sought. A contemplative nun cannot *prove* that her life is not wasted; she cannot point to the souls she has helped to save, the sinners converted, the babies baptised, and say, 'These are mine.' Life

---

[1] Col 1:24.
[2] Rom 6:10.
[3] cf II Cor 5:15; Eucharistic Prayer IV.
[4] Col 3:3–4.
[5] Jn 12:24.
[6] Gen 30:1.

is conceived and grows in hiddenness; 'the seed grows of itself'[1] in the dark, in seeming death. But unless there are those in the Church who are prepared to go down in the 'death' of faith to the darkness where life is rooted, the new growth of renewal above the surface of the ground will not be fed and will wither. It is the Spirit who renews the face of the earth, and he is poured out through the death and glorification of Jesus.[2] In the measure that contemplatives are united to their Lord in his Easter mystery they will be open to the Spirit and will be instruments in the renewal, the new Pentecost, for which Pope John prayed.

Listening to the word

The Church enters into the mystery of Christ as she listens to the word of God. The Spirit 'who spoke through the prophets' shaped the infant Church and her tradition, and inspired the life-giving word of the scriptures. This is not a dead letter but still the ever-new, powerful word of life for believers today, as it is proclaimed and listened to in the Church. Contemplative nuns seldom have occasion to proclaim it, but it is especially their role to receive it, like Mary who 'kept all these words, pondering them in her heart.'[3] In them the Church listens, humbly and prayerfully, ready to let the word take life and grow and judge. It is in this prayerful listening that theology is born, for the Church will never exhaust the mystery of Christ revealed to her through the Spirit who speaks in the scriptures. 'The tradition which comes from the apostles develops in the Church with the help of the Holy Spirit. There is a growth in insight into the realities and words that are being passed on. This comes about in various ways. It comes through the contemplation and study of believers who ponder these things in their hearts. It comes from the intimate sense of spiritual realities which they experience. And it comes from preaching…,'[4] This listening to the word in the heart of the Church is almost a description of the life of a contemplative nun.

---

[1] cf Mk 4:26 ff.
[2] Jn 7:39, 19:30, 20:19 ff.
[3] Lk 2:18, 2:51.
[4] Vatican II, *Dei Verbum* 8.

Only because her role is to *be* the Church – faithful to Christ, sharing his passover, led by his Spirit and listening to his word – is the nun honoured by the title given in scripture to the Church herself: Bride of Christ. And because the Church knows that her own vocation and her own inmost reality are mirrored and made present in the vocation of her contemplatives, Vatican II insisted on the need for contemplative presence in mission territories.[1]

CONTEMPLATIVE LIFE IN THE MODERN WORLD

God-hunger

Whether in mission countries or in the post-christian west, those called to contemplative life have withdrawn physically from the society of their fellow human beings only for the sake of a deeper spiritual involvement with the world and its needs. Thoughtful men today are searching for a meaning in life, for the secret of authentic human living, for true human community. They are restless and dissatisfied with materialism as an answer to the world's problems. There is wide-spread God-hunger, a longing for experience of God, a search for some kind of exposure to a reality that transcends man's achievements. 'Many people, including many of the young,' wrote Pope Paul in 1971, 'have lost sight of the meaning of their lives and are anxiously searching for the contemplative dimension of their being.'[2] For these the contemplative life, flourishing and encouraged by the Church, can be a witness to the reality of God, to his grace and the transforming power of his love, and to the fact that he is himself the ultimate satisfaction of the human heart.

The apostolate of hospitality practised in some contemplative houses can be a means of meeting this prevalent hunger for silence and

[1]'By their prayers, works of penance and sufferings, contemplative communities play a great part in conversions. For it is God who, in response to prayer, sends workers into his harvest, who opens the minds of non-christians to hear the Good News, and who makes the word of salvation fruitful in their hearts. Such communities are urged to found houses in mission areas.... Living out their lives in a way suited to the traditions of the people, they can bear splendid witness there among non-christians to the majesty and love of God, and to the brotherhood of men in Christ.' Vatican II, *Ad Gentes*, 40. cf ibid 18.
[2]*Evangelica Testificatio*, 45.

peace. Contemplatives may help by listening, counselling, and above all helping people to pray. Contemplative prayer, the quieting of all our faculties in a wordless attention to God and a receptivity to his love, is no prerogative of cloistered nuns, but should be an element in the life of every baptised Christian. Many people too who would not claim to be Christians are groping for it and need help and encouragement to persevere. Some of those who come in spiritual need to stay at contemplative monasteries may not be touched by any other form of the Church's apostolate, but will know with uncanny intuition whether a community is living a deep life of prayer.

Contemplative nuns have chosen to live at the heart of the struggle between good and evil which rages at every period of the history of the world but which has taken virulent forms in our day. The human family is perplexed with the problem of power, of how to control with wisdom the enormous forces placed by science at its disposal. But love is the mightiest source of power in the world, and because of the solidarity of mankind contemplatives believe that lives handed over to love can make a difference.

Can they prove it? No. A life given to God in that way is a venture of faith. They are like Moses who 'held to his purpose, as seeing him who is invisible.'[1]

---

[1] Heb 11:27.

Since the author is a Benedictine this pamphlet is inevitably written from a Benedictine standpoint, but an effort has been made to keep it general enough to be valid for other traditions too. What was said in the text about diversity of functions in the body of Christ is true also of the rich variety within the contemplative religious life, even in Great Britain. Though all share the role in the life of the Church outlined above, each order or congregation has its own emphasis, traditions and outlook, each is inspired by the memory and helped by the intercession of its own saints. A list of contemplative houses of women in England, Wales and Scotland is given below. It is confined to those which have no schools, though other communities not listed combine the contemplative spirit with external works. Further information can be obtained from *Directory of Religious Orders, Congregations and Societies of Great Britain and Ireland,* published biennially by John S. Burns & Sons, Glasgow.

ENCLOSED COMMUNITIES OF NUNS IN ENGLAND, SCOTLAND AND WALES

Adoration Reparatrice

    CHELSEA 28, Beaufort Street, Chelsea, London, S.W.3.

    LIVERPOOL 305, Edge Lane, Liverpool, L7 9LE.

Annunciades

    ST MARGARET'S BAY Annunciade Convent, St Margaret's Bay, Dover, Kent.

Benedictines

    (1) *English Congregation*

        COLWICH St Mary's Abbey, Colwich, Staffs.

        HOLME EDEN St Scholastica's Abbey, Holme Eden, Carlisle.

        STANBROOK St Mary's Abbey, Stanbrook, Callow End, Worcester.

        TALACRE St Mary's Abbey, Gronant, Prestatyn, N. Wales.

    (2) *Solesmes Congregation*

        RYDE St Cecilia's Abbey, Ryde, Isle of Wight.

(3) *Under Jurisdiction of Bishop of Diocese*

FERNHAM St Mary's Priory, Fernham, Faringdon, Berks.

HASLEMERE St Mary's Abbey, Haslemere, Surrey.

MINSTER Minster Abbey, Ramsgate, Kent.

OULTON Oulton Abbey, Stone, Staffs.

TEIGNMOUTH St Scholastica's Abbey, Teignmouth, S. Devon.

(4) *Congregation of Adorers of the Sacred Heart*

TYBURN Tyburn Convent, 8, Hyde Park Place, London, W.2.

WADHURST St Benedict's Priory, Beechlands, Wadhurst, Sussex.

Bridgettines

SYON Syon Abbey, Marley, South Brent, Devon.

Canonesses Regular of the Lateran

NEWTON ABBOT St Augustine's Priory, Newton Abbot, S. Devon.

Carmelites of the Teresian Reform

(1) *From Belgium in 1794*

LANHERNE Lanherne Carmel, Newquay, Cornwall.

CHICHESTER Carmelite Convent, Chichester, Sussex.

DARLINGTON Carmelite Convent, Darlington, Co. Durham.

(2) *From Lyons*

GOLDERS GREEN Carmelite Convent, Bridge Lane, London, N.W.11.

(3) *Founded from Notting Hill*

ST CHARLES' SQUARE Carmelite Convent, St Charles' Square, London, W.10.

BIRKENHEAD Carmelite Convent, Grosvenor Road, Birkenhead, L43 1UA.

BIRMINGHAM Carmelite Convent, 345, Church Road, Yardley, Birmingham, B25 8XR.

BRANKSOME Carmelite Convent, Branksome Park, Bournemouth.

BRIDELL Carmelite Convent, Bridell, Cilgerran, S. Wales.

DOLGELLY Carmelite Convent, Dolgelly, N. Wales.

DUMBARTON Carmelite Convent, Helenslea Road, Dumbarton, Scotland.

DYSART Carmelite Convent, Dysart, Fife, Scotland.

EDINBURGH Carmelite Convent, 4, Spylaw Road, Edinburgh.

FALKIRK Carmelite Convent, Falkirk, Stirlingshire, Scotland.

GLASGOW Carmelite Convent, Mansion House Road, Langside, Glasgow.

KIRKINTILLOCH Carmelite Convent, Kirkintilloch, Dunbartonshire, Scotland (founded from Glasgow).

LINTON Carmelite Convent, Wood Hall, Linton, near Wetherby, Yorks.

LIVERPOOL Carmelite Convent, West Derby, Liverpool, L12 9HY.

LLANDOVERY Carmelite Convent, Llandovery, Carmarthen, Wales.

OBAN Carmelite Convent, Oban, Argyllshire, Scotland.

OXFORD Carmelite Convent, 153, Banbury Road, Oxford.

PRESTEIGNE Carmelite Convent, Presteigne, Radnor, Wales.

PRESTON Carmelite Convent, Fulwood, Preston, Lancs.

QUIDENHAM Carmelite Convent, Quidenham, Norwich, Norfolk.

READING Carmelite Convent, 1, Southcote Road, Reading, Berks.

SAFFRON WALDEN Carmelite Convent, Saffron Walden, Essex.

SALFORD Carmelite Convent, Vine Street, Kersal, Salford, M7 0PS.

SHEFFIELD Carmelite Convent, Kirk Edge, Sheffield, S6 4LJ.

ST HELENS Carmelite Convent, Springfield, St Helens, Lancs.

TAVISTOCK Carmelite Convent, Tavistock, N. Devon.

UPHOLLAND Carmelite Convent, Upholland, Wigan, Lancs.

WARE Carmelite Convent, Ware, Hertfordshire.

WATERBEACH Carmelite Convent, Waterbeach, near Cambridge.

WOLVERHAMPTON Carmelite Convent, Penn Fields, Wolverhampton.

YORK Carmelite Convent, Thicket Priory, Thorganby, York.

Carmelites (Calced)

BLACKBURN Carmelite Convent, 11, Meins Road, Blackburn, Lancs.

Cistercians

STAPEHILL Holy Cross Abbey, Stapehill, near Wimborne, Dorset.

Dominicans of the Second Order

CARISBROOKE St Dominic's Priory, Carisbrooke, Isle of Wight.

GLASGOW St Dominic's Convent, 61, Hamilton Avenue, Glasgow, S.1.

Franciscans of the Third Order Regular Enclosed

WOODCHESTER Franciscan Convent, Woodchester, Stroud, Glos.

Passionists

DAVENTRY Our Lady of the Passion Monastery, Badby Road, Daventry, Northants.

Poor Clares

(1) *of the First Rule*

DARLINGTON St Clare's Abbey, Darlington, Co. Durham.

SCLERDER Sclerder Abbey, Looe, Cornwall.

(2) *Colettines*

ARUNDEL Convent of Poor Clares, Cross Bush, Arundel.

BADDESLEY CLINTON Convent of Poor Clares, Baddesley Clinton, Solihull, Warks.

BARNET Convent of Poor Clares, Galley Lane, Arkley, Barnet, Herts.

BLANTYRE Convent of Poor Clares, Blantyre, Lanarkshire, Scotland.

BULLINGHAM Convent of Poor Clares, Bullingham, Hereford.

ELLESMERE Convent of Poor Clares, Ellesmere, Shropshire.

HAWARDEN Convent of Poor Clares, Hawarden, Deeside, Flintshire.

LIBERTON Convent of Poor Clares, Lasswade Road, Liberton, Edinburgh.

LIVERPOOL Convent of Poor Clares, Green Lane, Missley Hill, Liverpool L18 2ES.

LYNTON Convent of Poor Clares, Lynton, N. Devon.

MANCHESTER Convent of Poor Clares, Clare Road, Levenshulme, Manchester.

NEATH Convent of Poor Clares, Neath, Glamorganshire.

NOTTINGHAM Convent of Poor Clares, Brooklyn Road, Bulwell, Nottingham.

SOUTHAMPTON Convent of Poor Clares, Bracken Lane, Shirley Warren, Southampton.

YORK Convent of Poor Clares, Lawrence Street, York.

Redemptoristines

CHUDLEIGH Redemptoristine Convent, Chudleigh, S. Devon.

Servites of the Second Order

BOGNOR REGIS Convent of Our Lady of Dolours, Hawthorne Road, Bognor Regis, Sussex.

Sisters of Jesus Crucified

CASTLE CARY St John's Priory, Castle Cary, Somerset.

Visitation Order

PARTRIDGE GREEN Monastery of the Visitation, Lock House, Partridge Green, Sussex.

WALDRON Monastery of the Visitation, Waldron, near Heathfield, Sussex.

WHY *ENCLOSED* NUNS?

Dom Bruno Webb OSB

WHY *ENCLOSED* NUNS?

Dom Bruno Webb OSB

'Of what use are enclosed nuns? What's behind the idea of such a life?' This is a question which has been repeated times without number, and the person, herself a nun, who asked me to write this pamphlet told me 'I could not tell you how often I have been asked, "Why did anyone as sensible as you, with all your experience, and able to do such a lot of good in the world, become an *enclosed* nun of all things? You who have lived in so many countries, spoken their languages, and obviously enjoyed it all—how *could* you lock yourself up like this? I could have understood it if you had become one of those nuns who go about doing good, but why shut yourself up where you can do no good to anyone?"' The same question is asked of those monks whose lives are confined to their enclosure, but perhaps less often since they are less numerous. But whether it be of monks or of nuns that the question is asked, the question is the same in both cases—'What do you *do* there?'

Why do they do it?

It is a perfectly sensible question to ask, and precisely because it is so sensible, and because it is so often asked, it deserves an answer. For thousands of non-Catholics who think about it at all, and to our shame we must admit for many Catholics who should know better, it is an enigma why sensible women with experience of the world, or gifted girls with all the sparkling charm of their teens, should turn their backs completely on the world and shut themselves within the 'gloomy walls'

23

of a convent. Whatever the motive which attracts them, is not this surely to waste precious lives which might so easily have been given to making others happier and better? Is it not a very selfish thing to do? Those who ask these questions are often perfectly sincere. Some of them look for an explanation in a morbid melancholia which leads its victim to shun the society of her fellow human beings. Or perhaps she has been thwarted in love, and is retiring to brood over it? Others, who have a closer acquaintance with those who have disappeared behind convent walls, realize that in many, perhaps in most cases they are either people endowed with an extra dose of balance and common sense, or are particularly high spirited and full of fun; and this will not tally with a morbid state of mind. But one and all realize that, whatever their motive may be, whether morbid or healthy, *some* motive there must be, and it is this that leaves them asking, 'What's behind the idea of such a life?' There must be some underlying reason, some key to the enigma.

I do not know what your experience is when watching a conjuring trick. I confess that in my own case it produces mental exasperation almost to breaking point. I feel tempted to think there must be a little devil spiriting this card away from here and putting that one there, since no human means could possibly do it; yet all the time I know it is just a trick. The exasperation comes from the frustration of the mind in being unable to see the clue, the principle on which the whole trick depends. Only once has a conjuror had compassion on me and shown me how it was done, and then I could scarcely credit not having seen it before. What appeared like magic was simplicity itself—once the *principle* on which it all rested had been seen. It is, I think, something of this mental frustration that so many experience when confronted with the enigma of the enclosed nun, because in this case too what the mind is seeking is the principle, the underlying idea why these girls so full of promise and with all the vivacity of youth, these common-sense women in the prime of life, cut themselves off from the world to become, apparently, useless to themselves or anyone else.

What of our Lord's own Life?

Now supposing we were to find the same enigma confronting us when we study our Lord's own life, what should we do then? We should no longer have to ask why do *they* choose such an obscure and apparently useless life, but why did He do so? On the other hand, if we can answer the question why He did it, shall we not be in a position to say why they still do it? And if He did it, can we any longer say it is a mistaken way of life? For He has said, 'Learn of Me…I am the way, and the truth, and the life'. If we reflect a little, what is the conclusion which forces itself upon us with regard to our Lord's life? Surely it is that the orientation of His life was primarily Godward and only secondarily manward. He who has so completely transformed the world spent only three out of thirty-three years, perhaps rather less, in external activity. The other thirty years were spent as an obscure carpenter in a remote hamlet of such little importance that Nathaniel, on hearing He came from it, exclaimed, 'Can any thing of good come from Nazareth?' His village shack was far more obscure than any twentieth-century convent, and was not His life at Nazareth equally 'useless'? Of what use to the world at large have been the wooden ploughs and tables that He made? Have they transformed the world? If He was to transform the world, should we not have expected a life brim full of activity, teaching, organizing and laying out plans, with every moment 'well filled'? Yet all we know of some nine tenths of His life is that 'He went down to Nazareth and was subject to them'. His life at Nazareth was hidden and obscure because it was directed, not toward men, but toward God.

Even during the three years of His public ministry He frequently retired into a lonely mountain to spend the whole night in prayer. And if we consider the one act of His life which, above all others, brought about the Redemption of the world, namely His Passion and Sacrifice on Calvary—what was this but a complete offering of Himself, on behalf of all mankind, *to the Father?* His sacrifice on Calvary was directed wholly Godwards, yet it is in answer to this supremely Godward act that God has received man back into His friendship which had been lost by sin. God is once again our Father and we are His children,

25

because Christ redeemed us on the Cross *by offering Himself to God* on our behalf. And if we are tempted to regard the enclosed life of monk or nun as useless, let us not forget that even the Cross itself is 'to the Jews a stumbling block, and to the Gentiles foolishness'. At least we must admit that the enigma is the same in both cases. Three short years only did our Lord spend in teachings preaching and 'going about doing good'. The enigma of the enclosed nun, therefore, has been transplanted into our Lord's own life.

Godward first

What conclusion, then, must we draw? Surely this, that if man turns Godward, God will turn manward. The Church's whole life centres round the Holy Sacrifice of the Mass which is the daily continuation of our Lord's supremely Godward Act, and the Church has always known this to be the mainspring of her life. What, then, did our Lord come on earth to do? He came, in the first place, *to give back to God*, on man's behalf, the obedience and worship which sin had denied Him. He came to acknowledge God's glory on behalf of all mankind, and *as the result of this* to regain for man the supernatural life of grace which sin had lost.

The majority of non-Catholics in this country have little if any notion of what is meant by grace or the supernatural order. Yet it is precisely the *supernatural* life of grace which is the key to the enigma both of our Lord's own life and that of the enclosed nun. It is therefore not surprising that those who do not understand what sanctifying grace is should also fail to understand the hidden life of our Lord at Nazareth or of the nun without her enclosure. We will, therefore, consider briefly what is meant by the supernatural life of grace.

The supernatural life of grace

What is the supernatural? It is nothing less than the raising up of our human nature so as to share quite literally in *God's own* Life through the free gift of sanctifying grace. St Peter, in his second Epistle, writes as follows:

'Grace to you and peace be accomplished in the knowledge of God and of Christ. Jesus our Lord…By whom he hath given us most great and precious promises; that by these you may be made *partakers of the divine nature.*' The uncreated Nature of God is infinitely above any possible created nature, whether human or angelic, yet St Peter says we are destined to partake of it. How can this be? A simple analogy may help us.

Consider a cable the moment before and the moment after it makes contact with its power station. Before contact it is a lifeless thing, but as soon as contact is made it is charged with a tremendous power capable of lighting up cities, running trains, and doing any other work that man may apply it to. It has become a 'live' cable; it has received a power which is something altogether new over and above the nature of the cable itself. This may help us to understand, however imperfectly, what the supernatural life of grace is. God is the power station in this case, and the live current which He produces in us is sanctifying grace which is itself the divine life imparted to us, permeating our nature throughout its whole being and raising it right above its natural level into the supernatural level of God's own uncreated Life. God has destined both man and angels to this supernatural life; sin consists in the refusal of it, and the salvation of a soul consists in its reaching its supernatural end by passing out of this world in possession of it into the blissful Vision of God.

From this short explanation one thing has become clear, that grace is *a completely gratuitous gift over and above anything to which our human nature can lay claim.* This is the meaning of the Latin *gratia,* hence our word gratis. It follows that no efforts of ours can produce grace, only God can give it to us. It is His free gift, and without it all our activities are powerless to produce any effect whatsoever towards the salvation either of our own souls or those of others. It is the great error of the world to-day that it is trying to do without God, and this error has infected the minds even of religious people so that they place all their faith in their natural activities, forgetting that these can produce nothing beyond their purely natural effects unless God charges them with His grace as the cable is charged with its current. For our activities to have any *supernatural* value they need this gift of grace which only God can give. 'Every best gift', says St James in his Epistle, 'and every perfect gift is from above, coming down from the Father of lights.' We may preach and teach and perform a thousand other works, but we shall do absolutely nothing towards the supernatural end for which God has destined us unless these activities are vitalized by God's grace. As St Paul says, 'If I speak with the tongues of men and of angels and have not charity. I am become as sounding brass or a tinkling cymbal… And if I should distribute all my goods to feed the poor…and have not charity, it profiteth me nothing.'

Please… Thank you

Once we realize that grace is God's completely gratuitous gift and that without all our activities are powerless to produce even the least supernatural effect, we shall understand why so much of our Lord's life was directed primarily Godward and only secondarily manward. If a father offers his little boy something very special, surely he expects 'please' or 'thank you', in fact both. And if he does not get these, surely he may and should say, 'Very well, you can go without it'. So it is with our heavenly Father who has endowed us His children with the gift of free will, and therefore demands of us free co-operation in His dealings with us. We must turn Godward first and foremost, for this is our 'please' and our 'thank you', if God is to turn manward with His priceless gift of divine grace. We must seek God before we seek our fellow men; if we do not we shall seek them in vain. God has promised that, if man will turn Godward, He will turn manward; and it is only when God turns manward with the outpouring of His grace that our works for others will bear any supernatural fruit. Our Lord has solemnly affirmed. 'Without me you can do nothing'; whereas, on the other hand, 'he that abideth in me, and I in him, the same beareth much fruit'. Grace is, as it were, the offspring of the union between a soul and God. The closer that union, the more fruitful it will be. This is the reason why it is the Godward action of the soul which *obtains* grace from God for the salvation of souls. However fruitful our external activities may be, it does not necessarily follow that it was we who obtained the grace which makes them fruitful. Our external activity may be no more than the channel *through which* grace flows, and that grace may have been won by the prayer of some unknown saint in the slums of one of our great cities or of some contemplative nun within her enclosure. For God can use anything as the channel of His graces, even irrational things like earthquakes and storms which 'put the fear of God into us'. In actual fact He makes use of everything that ever happens to us, because God's action upon us is continuous. But the graces which flow to us through all these diverse channels have to be won by somebody's 'please' and acknowledged by someone's 'thank you', and it is precisely in this *winning* of grace from God on behalf of mankind that the real work consists. Those who devote their whole lives to the praise of God, and so to the obtaining of grace on mankind's behalf, are doing the world's hard work for it. We are creatures endowed with free will, and God treats us according to the free nature which He has given us. Therefore, unless we co-operate with God by our Godward action, God will leave us to our own insufficiency and helplessness. The chaos in the world to-day all comes from man's effort to behave as though he were self-sufficient and in no need of God. If the world would go on its knees its troubles would be solved to-morrow.

The one thing necessary

Therefore the Church has always insisted that Mary has chosen, not only the better part, but *the one thing necessary.* The very complaint that is levelled against the enclosed nun to-day was levelled by Martha against her sister. 'But Martha was busy about much serving. Who stood and said: "Lord, hast thou no care that my sister hath left me alone to serve? Speak to her therefore, that she help me."' And did our Lord approve of this complaint? On the contrary, it drew from Him a rebuke. 'Martha, Martha, thou art careful and art troubled about many things; but one

29

thing is necessary. Mary hath chosen the best part, which shall not be taken away from her.' There you have our Lord's own estimate of the two kinds of life, that of the contemplative and that of the active worker. He does not condemn the latter, far from it but He does state which is in itself the better, and He does condemn those who complain of Mary's part. Yet what is better in itself is not necessarily better for this or that person, and some in an active order may be holier than others in a contemplative one. What matters for each of us is God's will, that we be *in that vocation to which God has called us* and in no other. The point is that the two kinds of life are designed for purposes as different as those of the heart and the hand; they are performing quite distinct functions within the organic unity of Christ's Mystical Body. How often the enclosed religious is asked, 'What do you *do* there?' There are many grades of activity. There is the material activity of the body, there is mental activity, and there is the spiritual activity of the soul or of an angel. But the activity of the spirit is an immensely higher and therefore more powerful activity than that of matter. If we deem it less, this is only because we cannot see it with our eyes. Prayer is activity of the soul as it were at white heat, hence the contemplative is doing more, not less, than if she were devoted to external activities, provided always that she is called by God to such a life. She is more active, not less.

But, you will say, that is all very well. I quite understand that this Godward attitude of the soul should take a large place, even the first place, in the lives of all of us; but why should there be people who do nothing else at all, and who cut out manward activity and any form of active apostolate beyond their enclosure altogether from their lives? Our Lord did not do this. This is a most important question, but if I am to answer it I must ask you to be patient while I explain something further. After that, I think you will see the reason why.

The Mystical Body of Christ

Our Lord said to His Apostles, 'I am the Vine, you the branches'. Now, between the vine and its branches there is identity. What, therefore, can this mean but that, in the supernatural sphere, we form a single living organism with Christ? St Paul, while he replaces the analogy of the vine with that of the human body, teaches the same thing. 'For as the body is one and hath many members; and all the members of the body, whereas they are many, yet are one body; so also is Christ. For in one Spirit were we all baptized into one body…For the body also is not one member, but many…Now you are the body of Christ' (I Cor. xii. 12-14, 27). Both analogies express the same truth that, in the supernatural order, Christ and the Church together are a single living organism. Christ is the fountain head and source of His Mystical Body the Church. We may compare Him to the original cell of the human body which is formed at conception. From that first cell the whole body develops, with its many distinct and highly specialized organs, each performing its own special function and all co-operating towards the good of the body as a single whole. There is the eye for seeing, the ear for hearing, the feet for walking, and so on with the rest. None of these is self-sufficient, but each contributes its own share towards the good of the whole. As St Paul says, 'If the whole body were the eye, where would be the hearing? If the whole were hearing, where would be the smelling? But now God hath set the members, every one of them, in the body, as it hath pleased him. And if they all were one member, where would be the body? But now there are many members indeed, yet one body. And the eye cannot say to the hand: I need not thy help. Nor again the head to the feet: I have no need of you' (I Cor. xii. 17–21).

Now, all these distinct and highly-developed organs are already present in a certain manner in the original cell from which the body grows forth. But they are not in that cell in an actually formed state as they are later on in the full-grown body. You would look in vain for them as distinct organs in the original cell before it has started to develop. Yet they really are in it though in a different manner. All those future organs are contained in it *virtually*; that is to say the original cell possesses the power to produce them as growth proceeds. The original cell is not specialized and so limited to a particular function such as are the cells of the eye, or ear or heart. Its energy is not given over exclusively to any of these, yet *it contains them all in embryo.* So it is with Christ and His Mystical Body. He is the original 'cell' from which the entire Church, His Mystical Body, has grown forth, and will continue growing till the end of time; so that Christ and the Church together constitute what St Augustine calls 'the whole Christ'. In the Church to-day we find many distinct 'organs' or ways of life, each highly specialized and given over to its particular kind of work, just like the different organs of the full-grown human body. There are orders for teaching, for nursing, caring for the poor, and so on almost without end. Though all these have their necessary background of prayer, they are, by the various ends characteristic of each, directed manwards: but there are other orders which give themselves exclusively to a life directed Godwards, to the praise of God and to intercession on behalf of all mankind. Our Lord, since He is, as it were, the original 'cell' of His Mystical Body, did not give Himself exclusively to any of these; His life was not 'specialized'. Yet virtually His life contained them all, since teaching, healing the sick, and the rest, all find their place in it: and above all He lived a life of prayer. But as the Church has grown forth from Him with the passage of the centuries all these elements in His life have become specialized into distinct orders and ways of life. So, just as we have orders of men and women which devote their energy to schools, or hospitals, like the specialized organs of eye or hand, so we have others which devote their entire energy to the Godward life of contemplation. This specialization is the law of growth, in the Mystical Body of Christ just as in the human body.

Are they selfish?

The idea that some people have that the enclosed nun is living a selfish life concerned only with saving her own soul is entirely false. It arises from ignorance of the doctrine of Christ's Mystical Body and of the supernatural solidarity of mankind in Christ its Head. For just as in the human body the health of one organ affects the entire body for good or bad, so it is in the Mystical Body. St Paul says, 'If one member suffer anything, all the members suffer with it; or if one member glory, all the members rejoice with it' (I Cor. xii. 26). Christ's Mystical Body is a perfect organism in which the health of one organ affects that of all the others. We cannot increase in virtue nor can we commit sin without raising or lowering the spiritual vitality of this Body throughout the world, and so affecting souls for good or for evil. It is never merely ourselves who gain by virtue practised, nor merely ourselves who suffer through consent to sin. So the grace which the contemplative draws down from heaven affects, not merely herself, but the whole Body throughout the world for, as St Paul says again, we are members one of another. Just as we may compare those who devote their lives to the external works of mercy to the visible members of the human body such as hands and feet, so we may compare the contemplative to the heart which remains hidden throughout life. The heart, by its continuous pulsations, sends the life blood coursing through the entire body, clearing away waste matter and rebuilding tissue; so by the continuous pulsation of their prayer these contemplatives send a ceaseless stream of grace coursing through the arteries and veins of Christ's Mystical Body throughout the world.

Prayer is the greatest power on earth

The power of prayer is not our own, but God's—'Ask, and it shall be *given* unto you'. To ask is the acknowledgement of our weakness; it is giving which presupposes power. So our weakness is answered by God's own infinite power when He gives grace in answer to our humble prayer. It is therefore a literal truth that prayer is the greatest power on earth, since nothing else can draw down God's own power. Furthermore, these enclosed religious come before God, not as mere individuals, but as members of Christ's Mystical Body who are specially consecrated to God by their religious vows, and by reason of this are deputed to represent the Church in an official capacity, to speak to God in her name as endowed with her God-given authority. We have already seen that the Church is Christ's Mystical Body, forming with Him 'the whole Christ', or, as St Thomas Aquinas says, 'one mystical Person'. But when a person speaks it is not merely his lips which speak, but *he* who speaks *through* his lips. So it is with these specially consecrated members of Christ's Mystical Body. When they act in their official capacity as members of Christ. it is not merely they who act, but Christ who acts through them. In some degree this is true of all practising Catholics, but especially of those consecrated by religious vows. They are the lips of Christ, and Christ continues through them that very same prayer, that perfect Godward Act which He performed on earth. Through them He perpetuates, as the centuries unroll, His twofold task of giving glory to God and of regaining grace for man. Since Christ is God Incarnate His prayer is infallible, it can never be unanswered, though it is not necessarily answered in the particular way we expect and hope for; yet it is this very prayer of His which passes through the lips of His members specially consecrated to this purpose. In answer to this prayer God pours grace upon the human race as the sun floods the earth with light, penetrating every crevice save where the stone-hard malice of a human will casts its dark shadow. And what is true of themselves as 'the lips of Christ' is true of the prayer round which their life centres. The Divine Office which they chant is the official prayer of the Church, that is to say of Christ's Mystical Body as such. It is therefore Christ's own prayer passing through the lips of the Church and, once again, Christ's prayer is infallible and all-powerful for the salvation of mankind save where sheer malice blocks the entry of grace into this or that soul. And at the centre of this prayer is the Holy Sacrifice of the altar which, as the Council of Trent tells us, is identical with the redemptive Sacrifice of Calvary save for the manner of its offering. Thus does the Redeemer of the world perpetuate through time and space the Godward action of His earthly life. And these contemplatives, by centring all the other occupations of their day, their reading and the labour of their hands whether in garden, field or workshop—occupations which so vividly recall those of the Carpenter of Nazareth—round this great Godward Act like the spokes of a wheel centred in their hub, are orientated continuously Godward like flowers which expose their entire surface to the life-giving rays of the sun. Thus filled with God, they themselves become centres of grace, microphones from which grace is radiated throughout mankind. We see what a state the world is in to-day—its conflict, its vice, its tyrannies. It has been trying to do without God, and this is the result of its supposed self-sufficiency. Nothing but grace can rejuvenate the world. Never were contemplatives more needed than they are to-day!

Old Testament types

There are certain passages? in the Old Testament which the Church is fond of using to illustrate the great power of the contemplative. You remember how Abraham besought God, who promised to spare the sinful Cities of the Plain if only ten just men could be found in them. Or again, how Moses on the hill-top lifted up his hands in prayer while Josue and his men fought the Amalecites in the plain below. 'When Moses lifted up his hands, Israel overcame; but if he let them down a little, Amalec overcame.' It is no longer a question of saving two cities from destruction or of defeating a mere army, but of a spiritual battle for the souls of men throughout the world; 'for our wrestling is not against flesh and blood, but against principalities and powers... against the spirits of wickedness in the high places'. The enclosed contemplatives hold up hands like Moses on behalf of a world that is forgetting God and is feverishly intent on using material measures to gain purely material ends, heedless of immortality and blind to spiritual forces that surround it on every side. 'It is easy to understand', wrote Pius XI in addressing the Carthusian Order, 'how they who assiduously fulfil the duty of prayer and penance *contribute much more* to the increase of the Church and the welfare of mankind than those who labour in tilling the Master's field; for unless the former drew down from heaven a shower of divine graces to water the field that is being tilled, the evangelical labourers would reap from their toil a more scanty crop.'

World wide like the radio

There is no limit to the sphere of the contemplative; her power is world wide, for there are no boundaries to the influence of prayer, no back alleys into which grace cannot penetrate. As the voice of the speaker hidden away in the broadcasting station travels everywhere, reaching the lowliest cottage out and beyond, so the grace generated by prayer penetrates the entire world, reaching its most remote and desolate souls save only those who refuse to 'listen-in'. Contemplatives, as Pius XI says, support the active apostolate, but they do more than this; as 'the lips of Christ' they plead the cause of those countless souls that no apostolate can ever reach. Every day as many souls pass through death's gateway as there are seconds in the day; and to how many of these do you suppose any active ministry of religion ever reaches? Yet none of these is beyond the reach of the contemplative's outstretched arms.

The work of the contemplative, therefore, is world wide, it is all-powerful save against final malice, but it is also a *hidden* work. We cannot see grace any more than we can see God, and only at the Last Judgement shall we know all that it has done. This is why so many people find it difficult to understand the tremendous work the contemplative is doing within her enclosure. But even in nature is it not true that it is the *hidden* things that do the most vital work? Which can you most easily afford to lose, external organs like feet and hands or even eyes, or the heart which ever remains hidden? It is not the cable which you can see, but the electric current which you cannot see that provides the power which lights up cities, drives trains, and sets in motion every kind of machinery. And what is more invisible than those electromagnetic waves which radiate the daily news?

'I am doing a great work'

It is because the work of these contemplatives is so supernatural and so hidden that the well meaning but less wise are always trying to induce them to undertake external activity and to 'make themselves useful'. You may remember the words of Nehemias when rebuilding Jerusalem, and his enemies were trying to frustrate his work by decoying him away to make a league with them. His answer was: 'I am doing a great work, and I cannot come down, lest it be neglected whilst I come and go down to you' (II Esdras vi). Of all works on this earth there is none which the devil detests more whole-heartedly than that of the contemplative. For he, 'as a roaring lion, goeth about seeking whom he may devour', and he knows that against the life of continuous prayer he is powerless. Therefore he sometimes seeks to deceive the contemplative herself by suggesting all the good external works she could do if only she will give up her life of prayer. How the devil is set at naught by those who are wholly given over to a life of close union with God! That is why he broadcasts so much misunderstanding of the contemplative life. It is because *he* knows its power that he would have us to think it useless. He knows to what extent his efforts to destroy souls are thwarted so long as there are 'ten just men' left in this sinful City of the Plain to hold arms upstretched before the Throne of Infinite Mercy.

The dominant note

One last word. If you are one of those who suppose that enclosed nuns are gloomy and long-faced, have done with it. If you think that, you have never known them. Close union with God does not produce melancholia, but joy. Joy is the hall-mark of all holiness; it is the dominant note which rings through the Church's liturgy, for the Church is ever merry with the joy of Christ. God is infinite bliss and joy, and it is impossible to live close to Him without becoming permeated with joy oneself. There may be much suffering whether of body or of mind, for those who share closely in Christ's own life must expect a share in His Passion too; but suffering and joy can go hand in hand as they did on Calvary. If you are looking for melancholic dispeptics you will find them in plenty of night clubs and other palaces of pleasure, where men and women are endeavouring to dope themselves against boredom and despair. But if you look for gloom within the convent enclosure you will be wasting your time; you are more likely to encounter the strength and good cheer of Benedictine peace, or what Mgr Benson has called the solemn joy of a Carmelite and the irrepressible gaiety of a Poor Clare. No, it is only a neo-pagan world that is forgetting how to laugh.

ENCLOSED COMMUNITIES OF NUNS IN ENGLAND & WALES

The following list is confined to communities without schools, etc.

ADORATION REPARATRICE (Perpetual Adoration of the Blessed Sacrament).

CHELSEA (28 Beaufort Street), London, S.W.3.

LIVERPOOL, 305 Edge Lane.

ANNONCIADES (Order of Our Lady).

ST MARGARET'S-AT-CLIFFE, near Dover. Kent.

BENEDICTINES

(1) ENGLISH CONGREGATION.

COLWICH, Stafford: *St Mary's Abbey* (Perpetual Adoration of B.S.).

HOLME EDEN, Warwick Bridge, Carlisle: *St Scholastica's Abbey.*

STANBROOK, Callow End, near Worcester: *St Mary's Abbey.*

TALACRE, Prestatyn, Flints, N. Wales: *St Mary's Abbey.*

(2) UNDER JURISDICTION OF BISHOP OF DIOCESE.

ATHERSTONE,Warwickshire: *St Scholastica's Priory* (Perpetual Adoration of B.S.).

HASLEMERE, Surrey: *St Mary's Abbey.*

MINSTER ABBEY, near Ramsgate, Kent.

RYDE, Isle of Wight: *St Cecilia's Abbey.*

TEIGNMOUTH, Devon: *St Scholasiica's Abbey* (Perpetual Adoration of B.S.).

(3) CONGREGATION OF ADORERS OF THE SACRED HEART (Perpetual Adoration of B.S.).

ROYSTON, Herts: *St Benedict's Priory.*

TYBURN CONVENT, 9 Hyde Park Place, London. W.2.

BRIDGETTINES

SYON ABBEY, Marley Head, South Brent. Devon (Day Adoration of B.S.).

CANONESSES OF ST AUGUSTINE

HODDESDON, Herts: *St Monica's Priory* (Day Adoration of B.S.).

NEWTON ABBOT, Devon: *St Augustine's Priory* (Perpetual Adoration of B.S.).

CARMELITES

(1) OF THE PRIMITIVE OBSERVANCE.

CHICHESTER (Hunston Road), Sussex.

DARLINGTON, Co. Durham.

LANHERNE, Mawgan, Newquay, Cornwall.

WELLS (11 Chamberlain Street), Somerset.

(2) OF CARDINAL DE BERULLE'S REFORM.

St Quintin Park (28 St Charles' Square, North Kensington), London W.10.

Golders Green (Bridge Lane), London, N.W.ll.

Highbury (64 Highbury Park), London, N.5.

Ashbourne, Derbyshire.

Berkhamsted (Woodcock Hill), Herts.

Birkenhead (Grosvenor Place, Oxton), Cheshire.

Birmingham (Church Road, Yardley).

Branksome (Leicester Road), near Bournemouth.

Bridell, Kilgerran, Pembrokeshire, Wales.

Cardigan, Wales.

Dolgelley (Cader Road), Merionethshire, Wales.

Exmouth (Keverel, Exeter Road), Devon.

Hitchin (Newlands Lane), Herts.

Liverpool (West Derby).

Llandovery, Carmarthenshire, Wales.

Newbury, Berks.

Oxford (153 Banbury Road).

Plymouth (Efford), Devon.

Preston (Garstang Road. Fulwood), Lancs.

Quidenham, Norfolk.

Reading ('Westfield', Southcote Road), Berks.

Saffron Walden (Ashdon Road), Essex.

Salford ('Moorlands', Vine Street, Kersal), Lancs.

Sheffield (Kirkedge).

St Helens (Eccleston), Lancs.

Tavistock (Spring Hill), Devon.

Upholland, Wigan, Lancs.

Waterbeach, near Cambridge.

Wolverhampton (Haddon Lodge, Poplar Road, Penn Fields), Staffs.

CISTERCIANS

Stapehill, Wimborne, Dorset: *Holy Cross Abbey.*

DOMINICANS OF THE SECOND ORDER

Carisbrooke, Newport, Isle of Wight: *St Dominic's Priory.*

Old Headington, Oxford: *All Souls' Priory.*

POOR CLARES

(1) OF THE FIRST RULE.

DARLINGTON, Co. Durham: *St Clare's Abbey*.

SCLERDER ABBEY, Looe, Cornwall.

(2) COLETTINE REFORM

ARUNDEL (Cross Bush), Sussex.

BADDESLEY CLINTON, Knowle, Warwickshire.

BAYSWATER (Westbourne Park Road, Notting Hill), London, W.11.

BULLINGHAM, near Hereford.

ELLESMERE (Otley Hall), Salop.

HAWARDEN (Aston Bank), Flints.

LEYLAND (Stanifield Lane, Farington), near Preston, Lancs.

LIVERPOOL (Green Lane, Mossley Hill).

LYNTON (Lee Road), Devon.

MANCHESTER (Clare Road, Levenshulme).

NOTTINGHAM (Brooklyn Road, Bulwell).

SCARTHINGWELL HALL, near Tadcaster, Yorks.

SOUTHAMPTON (Shirely Warren).

WOODFORD GREEN (128 High Road), Essex.

WORKINGTON (Park End Road), Cumberland.

YORK (St Joseph's Convent, Lawrence Street).

REDEMPTORISTINES

CHUDLEIGH, Devon.

SERVITES OF THE SECOND ORDER

BOGNOR REGIS (Hawthorn Road, South Bersted), Sussex: *Convent of Our Lady of Dolours.*

VISITATION ORDER

CASTLE CARY, Somerset.

For information regarding these and other communities, both men and women, the reader is referred to *The Religious Orders and Congregations of Great Britain and Ireland,* by Peter F. Anson (published by Stanbrook Abbey Press, 1949; stiff cover 12*s.* 6*d.*).

NUNS – WHAT IS SPECIAL ABOUT THEM?

Cardinal Daniélou

Profound changes evident

It is normal for religious life today to encounter problems. In a world such as ours, there have been some rather profound changes. It is normal that religious life itself would also encounter these questions. But what is important is that this encounter with contemporary problems results in an authentic renewal of religious life and not in its diminution or its deterioration. Actually, not only is there no reason why in a world like ours religious life should lose its importance or its characteristics, but because of the development of the material aspects of human life in today's world, it is all the more important that the spiritual dimension be represented in authentic fashion. From this point of view we ought to be profoundly optimistic in regard to the future which religious life will have in the technical and industrial civilization of today. But in order to do that, religious life must maintain its specific character. What I would like to point out briefly is the irreplaceable role of religious life in the Church and in society, and finally to indicate what is the proper mission of the woman religious today.

In the Constitution *Lumen Gentium* of Vatican II the place of religious life as a constitutive element of the Church is very clearly expressed. There is, as *Lumen Gentium* tells us, a diversity of functions in the Church, and in this diversity, religious life holds its own place. On the one hand, there is the function of the hierarchy, the function of the priesthood. This function is essential, since it is by the priesthood that the Church is constituted, and without priesthood, without hierarchy, there would be no Church. Practically speaking, what is the mission of the priesthood, the mission of the hierarchy? It is to be the instrument by which that action of God continues to be expressed among us, creating an atmosphere of truth, an atmosphere of grace which alone permits the development of the spiritual life. Religious life is a preeminent form of the development of the spiritual life, but there would be no religious life if there were no Church, no sacraments, and consequently if there were no priesthood.

Priesthood essential

Thus the priesthood is the first and essential condition for the existence of the Church, in so far as it is the instrument by which truth and grace are communicated. And from this point of view its role is absolutely essential. There can be no religious life without the sacraments. One of the aspects of religious life is its being an expansion of Eucharistic life. For where there is no priest, there is no Eucharist, there are no sacraments, there is no spiritual life.

The future of the priesthood, then, should be a great preoccupation of religious life, for it is certain that the present crisis in the priesthood constitutes a terrible menace to religious life. Without a priesthood that is conscious of its proper mission, which is primarily sacramental, there can be no spiritual life, and, therefore, no religious life.

On the other hand there is the function of the laymen, who have their own proper role in the Church. They are to render present the spirit of the Gospel in all the sectors of secular life. The role of the layman therefore is to penetrate the family, first of all, with the spirit of the Gospel—the creation of the Christian family is an admirable role and that of innumerable men and women. Further, their task is to render present the spirit of the Gospel in professional life, in the economic society of our time, and finally to give presence to the spirit of the Gospel in political life, that is, to bring ourselves, as the Sovereign Pontiffs have asked us to do so often, to have some of the spirit of Jesus Christ pass over into the organization of the City of Man.

Function of women religious

The function of women religious and the function of religious life is different from the function of priests and the function of laymen. It is different from the function of priests in so far as the function of priests is essentially that of being instruments by which grace is communicated. On the contrary, the function of religious is to render testimony to the fecundity of this grace communicated by the sacraments. I would say that from this point of view the sacerdotal life is more in the order of cause, for it is the instrument by which life is communicated, while religious life is closer to the end, for it manifests what are the marvellous effects of the grace which has come from Christ and which has been communicated by the sacraments. Religious life differs from that of laymen in so far as the essential role of the layman is to render present in the profane world the spirit of the Gospel. From this point of view laymen are essentially secular. On the contrary, the proper role of religious life is to testify to the fruitfulness of the life of the spirit in itself, essentially to be witnesses of the spiritual life and to manifest its splendour and its value.

It is very important to keep in mind that these conditions are complementary, that is, that each of them have need of the other. A Bishop at the Council one day was asked if the religious life was necessary for the Church and he answered: You can't say that religious life is necessary for the Church to exist, because in fact, when there is a Bishop and faithful in a region, the Church does exist. But rather religious life is necessary to manifest the development and the growth of the Church. The proof that the Church is doing well in a country is that it has generated religious vocations, and one can say that the Church is doing poorly if there are no religious vocations, because in this case then the Church has not realized its end, namely, that plentitude of sanctity to which religious life must testify. Furthermore, it is evident that the lay life has need of the religious life, in so far as the latter renders a witness to the primacy of spiritual goods, since the lay life, plunged as it is into the problems of profane life, always risks being drowned by them.

Secularism and clericalism

I would say that there are two dangers menacing religious life today: the first is that of secularism. To the degree that religious life is confused with the lay life, it does not achieve its proper end. A religious life which would simply be a witness of the Gospel in profane life is something which has lost all its specific character. After all, a good social worker, a good nurse, a good teacher who witnesses to the Gospel in his milieu does not have to be a religious to do that. It is evident that we must expect something entirely different from religious. It is precisely to bring out in relief the specific character of the spiritual life, the consecrated life, to manifest in a precise way by its transcendence what the life of the spirit represents itself.

There is another danger, one that I would call clericalism. It is the danger of turning the religious into the priest. This danger can come up in many ways. The first way would be that of women religious who dream of being priests. What religious really have to do is so beautiful in itself, that they really have nothing to envy the priest for, since in the Church each function has its value and its necessity. I would say that one of the great dramas that we are seeing in the Church today is that everyone wants to do someone else's job. The laymen want to be priests, and the priests want to play the role of laymen. At this point, nothing goes right and everything is in a state of confusion.

The other danger is more subtle, and certain theoreticians of religious life have sometimes been guilty of this. This theory says that religious life has no other end but to be at the service of priests, that is, that the religious would be basically a sort of inferior level of the priesthood, accomplishing the secondary tasks which the priests would give them. I do not in any way deny that religious can render service to priests and this is excellent. But this is not the finality of religious life. And this is why religious have to defend the specific character of their vocation when priests would simply like to use them for fulfilling the needs of their own diocese. When this happens, the conditions necessary for religious life would also be suppressed: common life, sufficient time for prayer, obedience in relation to one's superiors. Therefore, it is absolutely necessary that religious life in this area also maintain its specific character. Its essential purpose is to witness to the fecundity of the grace of Christ. It is not simply a second level of service to priests.

Role of religious life

I would say therefore that the problem in religious life today is a problem of identity, that is, that it is necessary for religious life to establish its specific character. We have to insist on this idea. It is only in this way that we will have well understood what is the irreplaceable role of the religious life, how much it is necessary for the Church and so absolutely necessary for the world, and how on the one hand we will be able to give ourselves to such a life with greater conviction, and on the other how we will be able to defend ourselves against anything that would tend to minimize its significance or to dissolve it into other spheres of ecclesial activity.

Our fundamental question, then, is what exactly characterizes religious life, and what characterizes the mission, the ministry of the woman religious in the service of the faith. At this point we have to draw back a moment in order to situate ourselves first of all in what the designs of God have in store for us. The design of God is essentially to raise up what I would call living spiritual beings. What I mean by this is that Christ has come to destroy the forces of death and sin by his passion, and by his resurrection to transfigure human nature, both ours and his, by filling it with the energy of the Spirit. The glorious humanity of our Saviour is even now the model of all living human beings. It is he who is the one who truly has life, for the true life is not the life of the body nor the life of the intelligence, but rather it is essentially the life of God transfiguring our human nature in all its aspects. What has been accomplished first of all in the flesh of Christ, in a body similar to ours, will tend to communicate the same thing to all flesh. The glorified Christ, exalted now at the right hand of the

Father, communicates his Holy Spirit, the Spirit with which he himself is totally filled, since the plenitude of God exists in him, and the Holy Spirit, communicated by him, springs up to life in our humanity in order to nourish all living human beings. It is precisely these people who constitute the actual reality of the Church, that is, this action of the Spirit which seeks to convert those hearts which are still caught in sin, which seeks to strengthen those who have come in contact with the Spirit, and which seeks to develop in them the life of grace. This is the admirable plan of God's love. It is the final answer to all the problems which men ask about their individual future and about the future of mankind in general. In a beautiful passage in Revelation, St. John the Apostle shows us a book sealed with seven seals which no one can open. And this sealed book is the one that holds the final secret of human destiny, a book which no philosopher nor any thinker has ever been able to open. And the Apostle weeps, thinking that no one can open the book. Then the angel answers him: Don't cry, for behold, here is the one who can open the book; and there appears the lamb offered in sacrifice, who is the only one who can open the hidden book of human destiny. It is he who at the same time unveils the meaning of our destiny in God's love, and also accomplishes in himself this very destiny, so that we have nothing else to do but simply to follow after him.

This is the admirable plan of God which has been announced to all men and which men have but to live.

God's plan of love

There are certain souls that the grace of God touches in a particular way, so that they are seized by a certain admiration in regard to the marvels which God has been able to accomplish in the souls of men, and so are led to consecrate themselves in a very particular manner to the realization of God's plan of love, that is, to the realization of the life of the spirit in themselves first of all, and then in others. I could say that there really is no other question but that one, for the religious life is essentially this total gift to the plan of God and to the service of his love, so that it is called, as such, a total consecration, whose foundation is admiration for the marvels which God has accomplished in this world. This means first of all that the religious soul is introduced, as it were, by the Spirit into this plan of God, that the soul seeks to understand it better, that the soul enters into this plan by the understanding of faith, and it is this aspect in religious life, this first aspect of the knowledge of God's plan and our adhering to this plan of God by faith, which is the foundation of everything.

This cannot be accomplished without a living faith, without a faith which develops into understanding, especially without a faith which touches the sovereign reality of divine things and which makes us know so deeply that there is something which is more real, and it is not that to which men attach importance, but is rather God himself and the things of God. This is exactly where religious life fits. Cardinal Newman, as we know from his *Apologia,* recounts how from his youth and from his adolescence, he had been overcome with the thought that ultimately two things existed: me and my Creator. The thought that God had separated him in some way from others to reserve him and to have him put at the centre of his life a sort of dialogue of love between God and himself, he said that this thought gave him the feeling of being a stranger to all the rest, so intense was this intimate relation of love. He adds—and this is very striking, because at the moment when he received this grace he was still an Anglican—that there was always one thing which was evident to him and that was to remain celibate. Sensing this choice of God on him, at no moment did he ever put in doubt that this choice implied for him to maintain this chastity as consecrated, a chastity which he felt was absolutely linked to the vocation that was his.

Work of the Holy Spirit

The Holy Spirit, therefore, first of all introduces the religious into a knowledge of the plans of God, giving the religious at the same time the understanding of his sovereign reality. And all of a sudden he draws it by a sort of love, of enthusiasm, by a movement towards that which God wishes to accomplish in the secret of the heart. The religious senses a suffering when he sees that God is not loved—and we know how when one is filled with love he wants to share this love. On the other hand, the religious experiences a deep conviction that is very intense, namely, that divine things are the only things that can truly nourish our heart. The Spirit inflames the divine charity in our heart, and what is religious life if it is not the development of supernatural charity in us, an intense love for God and for souls? From this moment on the Spirit arouses in us the desire to give ourselves totally to God in order to be the instruments of his marvellous designs. When we realize how much more marvellous is that which God wants to accomplish in us in contrast to what men want to accomplish, or how much more beautiful is the kingdom of God, more profound and more real than the construction of earthly cities, then how much more will our heart be attracted to give itself to Christ so that he can do with it as he will? It is this type of total dispossession which is visibly expressed by the vow of obedience which constitutes an essential element of our consecration to God, and is interiorly expressed by the need of docility to the Holy Spirit, by this desire not to accomplish one's own work or to have one's own success, or one's own personal development, but, on the contrary, to be totally at the service of the marvellous plan of God.

The heart of a religious experiences this intense reality of divine things, this admiration for the marvels which God has brought, and it desires to give itself totally to God by the religious consecration, to become an instrument itself of God's wonders. And this consecration is made by religious vows, by religious vows in their definitive form, for everything that is great is final. Marriage is final; the priesthood is final; religious life is final. It is one of the worst aberrations of our times to hear said that one can be a priest, a spouse, or a religious, for a time. This is the very denial of the gift. Under such conditions one would only be lending oneself, not giving oneself. This means one would remain one's own owner, reserving the right to take oneself back at will. What is essential in the religious vow is precisely that, by a definitive commitment, we are expressing this profound desire for being totally in the service of God in regard to all the eventualities of radical doubt, of questioning, and of temptation. It is a way of being sure that whatever the troubles that may be experienced, we have truly put our life at the service of the infinite plan of God's love.

Not of this world

This life which is totally handed over to God already achieves and anticipates that which is really the end of God's plan, namely, to raise up living spiritual beings; and this is why, moreover, among the saints, there shines forth something which is not of this world, which is not derived from flesh and blood, and which men really know in their hearts. We must keep in mind that in a religious life this begins in an inchoate manner and is developed over the years of a long life of fidelity.

There are those who ask the question: What conditions would enable the development of this life of the spirit, which could make possible this deepening of spiritual realities? This is precisely what makes a religious when she chooses to follow a rule. It is well known that from the moment that this desire of a total gift exists, there exists simultaneously the task of choosing those means which would make this gift possible. For it is evident—and this is one of those things that need repeating often, against certain errors of today—that the liberty of a human being is not something that can be exercised under any conditions. It is an absolute law of life that a man is dependent on the surroundings in which he lives. We know for sure—and it is a fact that is common knowledge—that some men, living in an atmosphere which is Christian, and carried by that atmosphere, will be faithful to the practice of the Christian life, but put them in an atmosphere that is hostile, and few would have the courage to be faithful to what they actually feel at the bottom of their heart. This does not mean that their faith is not a true faith. It does mean that the most sincere faith has need of being supported.

A religious Rule

What do we mean by the choice of a religious rule? It is that act by which, knowing that given over to ourselves we are capable of anything, and knowing that we would risk losing absolutely the best that we have experienced, knowing all this, we would choose those conditions which we know would support us, that would support our poor liberty, our poor weak will, and which would permit us to grow little by little. To think the opposite of this, to think that without a rule we could realize a spiritual ideal, is first of all a presumption, and secondly, pure stupidity. This would be totally to misunderstand the laws of human psychology. It is precisely in this area that we see in the name of a false concept of liberty, of false conceptions of what spontaneity is, in the name of a real caricature of the rule as something that oppresses or constrains us, when, in fact, it is really liberating—it is in the name of all these things that so often today we see religious challenging the Constitutions of their Order in their fundamental principles; or that we see a false liberty being substituted for these norms, a false liberty in which no spiritual life can truly develop. Let me give an example here: regularity in the exercises of piety and in particular in mental prayer. We know perfectly well, for all men are the same, that if religious, and especially young religious, are not supported by a rule, it is almost inevitable that, given the fluctuations of human mood, health and all that, there will develop an irregularity in the exercises of piety, and from that moment on there can be no spiritual progress. For there is only progress in something to the degree that we persevere in it, in spite of the vagaries of our mood and feelings. But someone who prays when he wants to, and who does not pray when he doesn't feel like it, will never make any spiritual progress. The universal experience of the masters of the spiritual life are agreed on this point. Thūs, any idea like this which would misunderstand the importance of this regularity, would absolutely put into question the possibility of any spiritual progress. And finally it is not a question that our women religious would just be good women, for there are many good people who are not religious. Nor is it sufficient to be simply good Christians—if only they were just good Christians! Religious life is at the same time important and fragile, and I insist on the latter: fragile, for the works of the Spirit are always vulnerable. A gross error of many men today is to believe themselves invulnerable, to believe that they can do anything, see anything, go anywhere, without risking the infinite delicacy of the works of the Spirit in the secret of their heart.

We have seen how the spiritual masters of the past possessed a different type of realism and a different prudence as if they knew exactly that if we want this fragile and precious flower to grow, a flower that the Holy Spirit has planted in our heart, in spite of all obstacles that could harm it—the temptations from within and the temptations from without—they knew that we would have to surround this little flower with a love of protection that would permit its development. Otherwise it would not grow, that is, there would be no true spiritual life. These religious would still be good women who live together, but from that moment on this religious life would not be worth the pain involved. And if it would only be that, it would be condemned to perish, for it would dissolve into certain devout and faithful forms of lay life, but which are not in any way religious life in its eminent dignity and in its great worth. What I mean to say here is that, besides the regularity on which I insisted a little while ago and which is the means by which the essential realities of religious life are protected from caprice and vicissitudes, there is also this prudence which the authors of the spiritual life call the custody of the heart, the custody of the senses, which alone can defend this fidelity to love, whose demands we know are very great. And where the sense of these demands has been lost, where there has been a sort of letting anything go, or of mediocrity, there will be no longer, from that moment on, any authentic religious life. It is from this point of view that the Constitutions of each religious order in their fundamental orientation—I am not talking about such or such an adaptation, for this is secondary; I mean what constitutes the principal elements—are the very condition for the spiritual life in religious life. Without this, it is an illusion to believe that such a life is possible. Moreover, what the rules of religious orders hold are, in the last analysis, a condensation of a centuries-old wisdom. This is one of the points that the Sovereign Pontiff has insisted on, showing how this was the experience of centuries, from the Fathers of the desert to the mystics of the Middle Ages, and to the great founders and foundresses of the orders of the 19th century, who, exactly assessing the laws of the spiritual life—for there are laws of the spiritual life just as there are laws in every other domain—have expressed, we could say, the quintessence of this wisdom in the rules which constitute the different religious orders. To misunderstand this, to think that we are all going to start from scratch, to believe that everything that came from yesterday is useless to the man of today because today's man is radically different from the man of yesterday, is one of the greatest illusions of a certain number of philosophers and theologians of today. And it is a total illusion, for what constitute the essential elements, namely, human nature and the spiritual life, are permanent realities. It would be particularly stupid to say that in the area of human genius we had made great strides since Plato, or since Dante, or since Shakespeare. That really would be stupid, for there is no progress in the qualitative order of genius. Bach and Mozart will always remain, because they have reached greater depths than certain modern works which grow old so quickly.

Sanctity does not change

Furthermore, to say that today we are holier than St. Paul, than St. Augustine, than St. Basil, is an enormous folly. Sanctity does not change. And this is why the writings of the great saints and spiritual men remain entirely useful for the people of today, and how much more real and current are they than so many superficial treatises which are in circulation today and which do not describe the realities of the spiritual life with the depth and the seriousness which are necessary.

Therefore, I would simply say that the spiritual life, the religious life, and the life of the religious woman, mean essentially being totally under the action of the Spirit, or tending to be totally under the action of the Spirit; and secondly, we cannot be under the action of the Spirit in a stable way unless we put ourselves in the context of certain conditions, that is, under a rule.

This is not to be understood by the woman religious as simply a seeking after personal perfection. This is also a mission in the Church, that is, by itself it brings to the Church something that is incomparable and which is absolutely necessary for the Church. First of all the woman religious enriches the Church on the level of personal witness. I mean to say that the first lesson, the first function of religious life is to witness, not to witness to what men are capable of, but to witness to that of which God is the author, that is, following the word of the Gospel: 'In seeing you, they give thanks to God.' I mean that there are things of which men are capable, for example, virtue, courage, generosity. And when men achieve these things, we turn to man and admire what he can do.

What is proper, however, to sanctity and to authentic spiritual life is that it is not the work of men, but is the work of the Spirit. That is, by the way, very encouraging, because this means that sanctity is conditioned by nothing else but faith, and that is why sanctity is possible for all men. You don't have to have special human talents. All that is necessary is to have a total faith and to give oneself over to the Holy Spirit. We have seen in history that there were some saints who felt themselves to be very weak individuals—St. John de Brebeuf said that he couldn't even entertain the idea of pricking his finger with a needle, and yet he was able to face the tortures which the Iroquois made him undergo, because he knew that at that moment the grace of God would come to his aid.

This is why the real object of religious life is to bring us in contact with that level of reality which is sanctity, that is, the order of being which only the Holy Spirit can accomplish in our hearts.

That certain humility

We can distinguish very clearly between a spiritual person and a virtuous person. They are not the same thing. There is in a truly spiritual soul a certain humility, because it knows that it is good for nothing and that the Spirit is responsible for all that it accomplishes. There is a certain docility to the Spirit, a taste for spiritual things, which brings forth in us, more than we would like to believe, the feeling that there is something in us that has come from God, that there has been a passage of God in us. And this is what religious life testifies to, as I said in the beginning, to the fruitfulness of grace in a soul, to those marvels which God can accomplish in the souls of those who give themselves to him.

On the other hand, there is a form of witness which is not just interior, but also exterior. And this is perhaps the difficult point, the most difficult point, because it is the most contested in religious life today. We are in the presence of a frame of mind among a certain number of theologians, philosophers, and others, who tell us that we are in a world that has been secularized and desacralized. By this they do not mean that it is not possible to have an interior relationship with God. What they do mean is that this personal interior relation should not have an exterior sign, and that, moreover, we should get rid of these visible signs. This is evident in many areas of life today. For example, I heard a priest say that 'to build a Church today would be a manifestation of triumphalism'. They say we should not want to manifest ourselves so visibly, that we should just be content to have a room which can be used for meetings, or for conferences, and where we can say Mass from time to time. They mean by this that the modern city should be a city that is totally secular and that the presence of God ought not to be expressed visibly anymore.

I can see today that many venerable customs of the Christian family, such as putting a crucifix or an image of the Blessed Virgin on the wall or saying prayers in common—all these things to which children are so sensitive and become so attached—all this is tending to disappear, always with the idea that it is no longer necessary to manifest in a visible way what exists interiorly.

One of the aspects of this desacralization and of this destruction of signs is the disappearance of the religious habit. And we should keep in mind here that this aspect is a real part of a whole way of thinking, and it is only one particular aspect of a whole, namely, a massive aggression of a world that has been secularized.

We have to say that this is a very great error. Those who, twenty years ago, were saying that we are going towards a desacralization of society, are rediscovering today that the need for the sacred is something so profoundly rooted in the heart of man that it will spring up all over again.

In the presence of a boredom which is the result of a purely technocratic civilization, purely orientated towards that which is useful, we see today the revolt of many young people, a revolt sometimes filled with aberrations, but because of a profound need they demand celebrations, ask for a visible expression, form among themselves on the margin of society groups of prayer or of charism. We see a writer like Harvey Cox, who wrote *The Secular City* and more recently *The Feast of Fools*, tell us in his latter book that the modern world has need of celebrations and need of temples.

Behind the times

Today the streets of our cities are filled with religious Hindus, Koreans, Chinese, who wear magnificent outfits, while our own religious wear no habit. We have to say that the idea of desacralization is an idea that has already been condemned, and that only those minds who are really behind the times would condemn the religious costume. The religious habit is a prophetic act and not a leftover from the past, that it expresses an actual need of humanity today. We must be all the more convinced that what religious represent is not a defence of the past. What we are interested in is the conquest of the future, and you must be persuaded that it is precisely this integral fidelity to religious life which will dominate the future and which finally will be the last word in the face of all attempts to secularize.

This completes the aspect of how interior and exterior witness is given. Certainly, the penetrating power of the religious life does not stop there. It manifests itself also in the irrepressible need to share what we ourselves live. One cannot love without desiring to share that love. And in this aspect, certainly, one of the parts of the mission of the woman religious in the Church is to share with others what she herself lives. This means not only to penetrate the meaning of spiritual things, but to try to lead others also to penetrate the spiritual meaning. Here we have to recognize that, in no matter what fashion, there are in religious life an action and a testimony which are absolutely different from that which laymen could give in the face of the great human realities: in the face of death, in the face of suffering, in the face finally of the spiritual misery which is deeper in humanity than the wretchedness of the body. The woman religious has the precise task of communicating this spiritual mercy, of having pity on souls. Let me repeat here again that one of the aberrations of the contemporary world is to put all the weight on temporal charity, on a charity whose only concern is the material amelioration of man's condition, by social action, by political action, by cultural action. All this is good, but there is nothing specifically Christian about this. Atheists also do this. We are not the exclusive specialists in charity, in the sense that we would call ourselves specialists in dedication—this would be hypocrisy, for there are atheists who are perfectly dedicated.

The most divine thing

That which is specific to the charity of Christ is that it is a charity which does not simply see human problems, but which brings about in others what the Spirit hopes to realize, which co-operates with the action of the Holy Spirit in the Church. This is what we can call the apostolate, and what we could call mission. It is the co-operation with the work of the Holy Spirit.

To co-operate with God in the salvation of souls, said a theologian whom we call Dionysius the Areopagite, is, of all divine things the most divine itself. Nothing is more divine than to co-operate with the Holy Spirit to develop the spiritual life. It is clear, however, that no one will seek to encourage the spiritual life, if he himself does not have a taste for the spiritual life. The mouth speaks from the abundance of the heart. Anyone who is filled with God will speak of God; someone who is empty of God will not speak of God or will speak of him poorly.

This is to say that the apostolate is a superabundance of our own contemplation, like a superabundance of love, a need to share what one has lived oneself. This is the mission of the woman religious. Her ministry is simply the expansion of what she has achieved herself first, or is trying to realize in herself, namely, the divine life.

Sacramental life essential

Let us say in conclusion that this cannot be accomplished except in the Church and in union with Christ. I said previously that the role of the priest is to create that atmosphere of grace by sacrament and by word because it is only in this atmosphere of grace that the life of the spirit can develop. Christ has given his Spirit to his Spouse, the Church, and thus it is in the Church and in our union with the Church, a union which should grow greater, that we will find the conditions necessary for the Spirit to work in us. This is true, first of all, for sacramental help. I want to add here how important it is that religious remain faithful to the sacramental life in its totality, especially at a moment when the sacramental life itself is menaced, at a moment when there is a disaffection for the sacramental life. There is no sanctity, there is no religious life, outside of the Eucharist. We can say that the religious life is the expansion of those energies which the Eucharist has developed in us. I would add that this love of the Blessed Sacrament should not only be expressed in the Mass, but should also be expressed in the veneration of the Blessed Sacrament, by visits to the Blessed Sacrament, by adoration of the Blessed Sacrament, by many of those things which some people today have abandoned and have let fall into disuse, but which have been and will remain for always the incomparable sources of the spiritual life.

We can mention the importance of the Sacrament of Penance, which is so vital in developing the purity of intention which should be found among religious, the purity of heart, the purity of conscience. Without this purity of conscience, of intention, of heart, there can only be rough work accomplished. For it is exactly at this point that love becomes active, that we see in action the perception of those divine things which are being accomplished. Today we are faced with a great depreciation of the Sacrament of Penance. The Constitutions of all religious orders give it a place of great importance. It is one of the means of the spiritual life, a means which is most important, and it would be terrible to see it neglected or allowed to fall into disuse.

We cannot base an authentic religious life on erroneous theological opinions. One of the greatest threats to religious life today is the mass of disputable theological opinions. In minimizing the supernatural aspect of God's gift, in minimizing everything that pertains to the action of the Spirit, they destroy the very base on which the religious life is built. That is why it is important today to seek our spiritual directors and theologians from those who represent the true thinking of the Church. There must be a care to have a deep unity with the Sovereign Pontiff and with the orientations given by the Sovereign Pontiff, in particular those which concern religious life.

In a troubled period like our own, the responsibility for religious life in the Church is a grave one. I mean that the worst corruption comes from things that were excellent. To the degree that a faithful and fervent religious life is beneficial for the Church, to the same degree a degraded or denatured religious life is detestable. It is painful to hear bishops say that in their dioceses it was often the religious first who were the ones responsible for the harm that is being done, and from there it reached the priests and the people. This should make us realize our great responsibility. It is really the good of the Church which is at stake. The renewal of the religious life has always been, in the history of the Church, the departure point for the renewal of the Church. The corruption of the religious life—look at the sixteenth century—has always been one of the signs of the decadence of the Church. This fidelity which is demanded of religious is not only for their sakes, or to defend a life that is dear to them, but rather this fidelity is needed for an authentic service to the Church, and that is why it is asked of us.

BACKGROUND

Maria Boulding was a highly-respected spiritual writer and translator, notably of St Augustine. Her testimony, as a contemplative nun, is eloquent and forceful: "love is the mightiest source of power in the world, and because of the solidarity of mankind contemplatives believe that lives handed over to love can make a difference".

Bruno Webb's text, from a generation earlier, is more theoretical, although with a robust sense of the reality of enclosed life.

Jean Daniélou wrote in the immediate aftermath of the Conciliar reforms, and the wholesale recasting of much religious life. He insists the religious vocation depends on unfashionable elements such as formal prayer, living under obedience, wearing a habit: these are both prophetic signs and an essential framework to allow God's grace to work unhindered by our egotism. The vocation is expressed primarily in the experience of loving God and being loved by him. It is to this that contemplative nuns above all are called.

CTS ONEFIFTIES

1. FR DAMIEN & WHERE ALL ROADS LEAD · *Robert Louis Stevenson & G K Chesterton*
2. THE UNENDING CONFLICT · *Hilaire Belloc*
3. CHRIST UPON THE WATERS · *John Henry Newman*
4. DEATH & RESURRECTION · *Leonard Cheshire VC & Bede Jarrett OP*
5. THE DAY THE BOMB FELL · *Johannes Siemes SJ & Bruce Kent*
6. MIRACLES · *Ronald Knox*
7. A CITY SET ON A HILL · *Robert Hugh Benson*
8. FINDING THE WAY BACK · *Francis Ripley*
9. THE GUNPOWDER PLOT · *Herbert Thurston SJ*
10. NUNS – WHAT ARE THEY FOR? · *Maria Boulding OSB, Bruno Webb OSB & Jean Cardinal Daniélou SJ*
11. ISLAM, BRITAIN & THE GOSPEL · *John Coonan, William Burridge & John Wijngaards*
12. STORIES OF THE GREAT WAR · *Eileen Boland*
13. LIFE WITHIN US · *Caryll Houselander, Delia Smith & Herbert Fincham*
14. INSIDE COMMUNISM · *Douglas Hyde*
15. COURTSHIP: SOME PRACTICAL ADVICE · *Anon, Hubert McEvoy SJ, Tony Kirwin & Malcolm Brennan*
16. RESURRECTION · *Vincent McNabb OP & B C Butler OSB*
17. TWO CONVERSION STORIES · *James Britten & Ronald Knox*
18. MEDIEVAL CHRISTIANITY · *Christopher Dawson*
19. A LIBRARY OF TALES – VOL 1 · *Lady Herbert of Lea*
20. A LIBRARY OF TALES – VOL 2 · *Eveline Cole & E Kielty*
21. WAR AT HOME AND AT THE FRONT · *"A Chaplain" & Mrs Blundell of Crosby*
22. THE CHURCH & THE MODERN AGE · *Christopher Hollis*
23. THE PRAYER OF ST THÉRÈSE OF LISIEUX · *Vernon Johnson*
24. THE PROBLEM OF EVIL · *Martin D'Arcy SJ*
25. WHO IS ST JOSEPH? · *Herbert Cardinal Vaughan*